From the Farm to the Table
Alpacas

Nonfiction 2-3 Grade Picture Book on Agriculture

by

Kathy Coatney

CONTENTS

Dedication

To Farmer Scott,
with thanks for his
time and expertise.

Acknowledgments

Many thanks to those who have assisted me with this project. Georgia Bockoven, who put the idea in my head. To my email check-in pals, Jennifer Skullestad and Lisa Sorensen, a huge thanks. Luann Erickson, Susan Crosby, Karol Black, and Tammy Lambeth, who critiqued and supported me through the process. To my family, Nick, Wade and Devin, Collin and Ellis, Jake and Emily, Allie and Russell. You all have been my inspiration. Thank you. I never would have made it without you.

Note to parents and teachers: The words underlined are second-grade vocabulary words. A list of the words used can be found at the end of the book.

Also By

Thank you for reading **From the Farm to the Table Alpacas**, book 7 in **From the Farm to the Table** series of picture books.

I love hearing from my fans. You can contact me through my website: www.kathycoatney.com.

From the Farm to the Table

From the Farm to the Table Dairy
From the Farm to the Table Bees
From the Farm to the Table Olives
From the Farm to the Table Potatoes
From the Farm to the Table Almonds
From the Farm to the Table Beef
From the Farm to the Table Alpacas

Box Sets

From the Farm to the Table: Almonds, Bees, & Potatoes
From the Farm to the Table: Olives, Beef, & Dairy
From the Farm to the Table: Bees & Almonds
From the Farm to the Table: Dairy & Beef
From the Farm to the Table: Olives & Potatoes

Dad's Girls

From the Farm to the Table Alpacas

Farmer Scott at Crescent Moon Ranch.

Farmer Scott raises alpacas on the Crescent Moon Ranch in Terrebonne, Oregon. It is called an agritourism operation meaning the public can <u>tour</u> the ranch, see the animals, and even buy things on the farm.

Alpacas at Crescent Moon Ranch.

The high country in South America is the natural <u>habitat</u> of alpacas. They were first imported into the United States in 1982.

Yarn from an alpaca on Crescent Moon Ranch
sold at The Alpaca Boutique.

Farmer Scott and Farmer Debbie
(his wife) have been raising alpacas
since 1996, which is almost thirty
years. Besides the alpacas on the
ranch, they have a store on the
farm called The Alpaca Boutique
that was an old potato <u>cellar</u>.

Huacaya alpacas at Crescent Moon Ranch.

There are two breeds of alpaca, the Suri and the Huacaya. Farmer Scott used to raise both breeds of alpacas, but now he only raises the Huacaya. Less than 10 percent of the world's alpaca population are the Suri breed.

Huacaya alpacas grazing.

The difference between the two breeds is the kind of fleece they grow. Huacaya fleece grows straight outward from the skin and Suri fleece grows out and hangs down from the skin. The two fleeces make different products.

Baby alpaca at Crescent Moon Ranch.

Adult alpacas weigh between 100-190 pounds. A newborn alpaca typically weighs between fifteen and twenty pounds.

Alpacas at Crescent Moon Ranch.

Alpacas make a variety of sounds. When they are in danger, they make a high-pitched, shrieking whine or a "bugling" noise when they feel threatened. When they are being friendly, alpacas will make a "cluck," or "click" sound.

Rachel Leason and her daughter, Clara, with Nicaeus. Photo courtesy of Scott Miller.

The alpacas on Farmer Scott's ranch are raised for show, meaning they are judged against other alpacas on their conformation (the proportions and correctness of their bodies), the structure and volume of their fleece, and the quality of it.

Scott and Debbie Miller, owners of Crescent Moon Ranch with Emmaus. Photo courtesy of Scott Miller.

Each alpaca competes against other alpacas of the same color, age, and gender. Winners are selected on conformation and fleece quality, which includes uniformity of crimp (or the amount of wave in the fleece), fineness, density, and color throughout the fleece.

Farmer Scott mowing the grass.

Farmer Scott has many <u>chores</u> every day. In the summer, the very first thing he does is move the sprinkler <u>irrigation</u> from one pasture to another so that each pasture stays green and healthy for the alpacas to eat. He also has to mow the grass.

Farmer Scott raking manure for the compost pile.

There are about 200 alpacas on the ranch, and they make a lot of manure or poop so the second <u>chore</u> for Farmer Scott is to clean up all the manure in the field and barnyard. It takes most of the morning to complete this task.

14

A compost pile that will be spread on the hay field in the winter at Crescent Moon Ranch.

All manure is moved to one area where it is composted. It's spread on the hay field as fertilizer in the winter. During the winter months, the alpacas are in the hay fields. In the summer, they are in the pastures.

Alpacas grazing.

Alpacas <u>prefer</u> to be with their herd. When visitors come to <u>tour</u> the ranch, alpacas will leave the herd if they are offered grain to eat.

Alpaca at Crescent Moon Ranch.

In South America, alpacas are used primarily for fleece and food, but Crescent Moon Ranch shows and sells alpacas as well as shearing them for fleece.

Alpacas eating grass and hay.

Alpacas eat continually throughout the day, but they only eat small amounts—much less than cows or horses or sheep. Alpacas often eat hay and grass, but they <u>especially</u> love grain pellets for treats!

An alpaca posing for the camera.

Alpacas have what is called a three-chambered stomach, and combined with chewing cud, it allows the maximum removal of nutrients from low-quality feed. Chewing cud is the process of slowly chewing food over and over before swallowing.

Alpacas grazing.

   Food can stay in an alpaca's first stomach for up to sixty hours and ferment (make a chemical change).

Alpacas eating hay and grain in the barn.

At Crescent Moon Ranch, the alpacas are brought into the barnyard every night and fed hay. They are also <u>examined</u> to make sure they don't have any health problems or injuries. If there are issues, Farmer Scott treats them.

Baby alpaca.

Female alpacas have a baby or *cria*, which means baby in Spanish, every year. There are 70-75 baby alpacas born on the ranch yearly.

Baby alpaca nursing.

Alpacas are pregnant for 11-12 months and usually have one baby that weighs about 15-20 pounds at birth. Twins are extremely rare. Unless there are complications, alpacas don't need help delivering their babies and <u>prefer</u> to be left alone.

Alpaca showing off her teeth.

All the alpacas at Crescent Moon Ranch are given names. At birth they are referred to as Sadie's baby or Agnes' baby, but at about six months, they have blood drawn, are microchipped, and named.

Baby alpaca grazing.

Baby alpacas gain approximately a pound a day when they're growing.

Baby alpaca fleece from first shearing.

The *crias* are sheared midsummer, but their fleece doesn't become usable until the second shearing. Shearing is when they cut the fleece from the alpacas. The first shearing is done for health and more uniform fleece in their second shearing when they are a year old.

Farmer Scott holding a baby alpaca.

At Crescent Moon Ranch, the *crias* start <u>arriving</u> in early March with a few more in April. Another batch arrives in May through early July. The alpacas at Crescent Moon Ranch stop having babies in the middle of September, but alpacas can have babies all year long.

Alpacas cooling off at the sprinkler.

Alpacas are very adaptable animals. They do well in the cold climates, and they actually seem to enjoy the cold. The heat doesn't bother them, either, but they don't seem to be as comfortable when it's hot.

Alpaca resting in the pasture.

Most alpacas live to be fifteen to eighteen years old. As the alpacas age, their fleece declines and becomes shorter and coarser than younger alpacas. The older fleece still makes great products.

Adult fleece. Photo courtesy of Scott Miller.

Each alpaca provides a different amount of fleece. Some alpacas can grow over fifteen pounds of fleece per year while others only grow four to five pounds. The Huacaya's fleece has a light and soft texture.

Adult alpaca fleece. Photo courtesy of Scott Miller.

The adult alpacas are shorn in May. Shearing is stressful for the animals so it's done in cool weather. The fleece from each alpaca is placed in a bag so that they know which fleece is from which animal.

Farmer Debbie showing the yarn made from alpaca fleece.

The fleece is shipped to a mill in Idaho. At the mill, the fleece is cleaned and spun into yarn, then shipped back to the ranch where Farmer Debbie sells it in the store.

Alpaca posing for the camera.

Unlike sheep's wool which requires chemicals for processing, alpaca fiber is cleaned with soap and water. This is much better for the environment.

Scarves made from alpaca fleece.

Alpaca fleece is as soft as cashmere, but warmer than wool, hypoallergenic (meaning most people don't react to it), and it is water-resistant.

Farmer Scott with his alpacas.

Raising alpacas is a commitment, but it's also a labor of love for Farmer Scott. He would much rather be out with his alpacas than in front of a computer. He says there is nothing better than being outside with his own herd of alpacas seven days a week.

The End

Vocabulary List

Arriving
Cellar
Chore
Climate
Especially
Examined
Habitat
Irrigation
Prefer
Tour

Author Biography

Kathy Coatney has worked as a freelance photojournalist for thirty-five years, starting in parenting magazines, then fly fishing, and finally specializing in agriculture. Her work can be seen in the California Farm Bureau magazine, Ag Alert and West Coast Nut magazine.

Kathy also writes a series of nonfiction children's books, From the Farm to the Table and Dad's Girls.
She loves to hear from her readers and always loves suggestions for future books.

Visit her website at:
www.kathycoatney.com or by email
kathy@kathycoatney.com.